DAVID WELLER

Storytelling for Language Teachers

Story activities, techniques and frameworks

Contents

V Final Thoughts

I

Stories & Learning

1

The Power of Stories

When I started teaching in 2003, in a school in the middle of China, no one used stories to teach.

Every coursebook unit had a story for students to cut out and fold into a booklet, but my colleagues ignored it. They were under pressure to spend more time teaching the unit's vocabulary and grammar. So what did I do?

I followed the lead of my seniors. After all, I was a fresh new teacher who knew no better. Then, one day in my second term, I had a particularly smart class that finished a unit much faster than expected. I was in the middle of a lesson, with one hour to go, and nothing was left in my plan. In desperation, I used the story to fill the time.

It was revolutionary.

We sat in a circle on the floor, looked at the booklet cover, and talked about what they thought the story would be about. We read the story aloud using silly voices, laughed at the characters and talked about the ending. They repeated in pairs (including the silly voices!), discussed the story's events and wrote alternate endings for homework. The lesson was fun–for them and me. Every student completed their homework on time, to an excellent standard (a first!).

I knew I was onto something.

Stories clearly worked for student motivation; that much was obvious. But did they work for language development? I had to find out. I used stories with other classes, researched different ways to use stories and (to cut a long story short) I saw a huge improvement in my students' progress when I used stories regularly.

In the twenty years since then, I've used various teaching methods and techniques, but I keep returning to stories. I've refined different story techniques, activities and methods to bring the power of stories to every student - young, old, beginning and advanced. Whenever I use stories, students are more engaged and progress faster. Younger students behave better, teenage students are more willing to talk, new students are less shy, and advanced students stay motivated.

Now I want to share these secrets I've learned with you so you can do all this too.

Who is this book for?

It's for language teachers looking to harness the power of stories. It's for teachers who know there must be an easier way to use stories but aren't sure where to start. It's for teachers who can never remember stories, who don't know where to find stories, and who don't know any story activities. You only need to have the desire to help your students learn faster and make your lessons more enjoyable.

Which age groups can I use this for?

It's for all ages. Young learners soak up stories, but they're equally valuable for older students, (although they can have stronger preferences about the stories they like). But really- everyone enjoys a good story.

What's the best way to use this book?

This book has five sections:

- **Part I** examines why stories are so powerful, and the science behind stories and learning.
- **Part II** discusses where to find, adapt or create stories, plus common story elements and frameworks that belong in every teacher's toolkit.
- **Part III** shares a step-by-step method for preparing and improving any story to use in class, storytelling techniques, and how to assess student progress.
- **Part IV** is a huge selection of story activities. Most are highly adaptable and can be used with different language aims and student levels.
- **Part V** ends with some storytelling do's and dont's, and final thoughts.

Good luck, and enjoy your storytelling!

2

Why Stories?

Storytelling is in our bones.

Stories help us make sense of our world and our place in it.

From the earliest days of humanity, stories have been used to entertain and educate. Stories passed on cultural values, traditions, and moral guidance. Sometimes the teachings are explicit ("Don't lie or the wolf will eat you!"), and sometimes hidden. As psychologist Jonathon Haidt says, the human mind is a story processor, not a logic processor.[1]

Stories also build rapport and empathy. We can't help but be changed when we hear a good story. We listen, we relate, and we can see ourselves in the characters and identify with the events and experiences they are going through. This builds a connection between the storyteller and listeners (and between listeners as well).

Stories also help us remember. As we listen to a story, our minds create images, sounds, and emotions, giving us mental "hooks" to hang our memories on. This makes stories the perfect vehicle to pass on knowledge.

Stories change with time, even though the core often stays the same. Over time, we adapt stories for different audiences, messages and contexts. Teachers can adapt age-old tales to match our students' interests and language levels to convey a particular message. This adaptation makes sure the story is both relevant and interesting for our learners. Stories evolve and endure, bridging the gap between the past, the present, and the future.

3

The Science of Storytelling

Stories are fun. But can they really help students learn a language?

Luckily, stories have come under scrutiny over the years. Educators and researchers have conducted many studies on how stories affect language learning outcomes.

Let's jump in and look at some of the findings.

It appears that cognitively, stories are crucial for making sense of the world.[2] They function as mental maps (known as schemata), providing us with a structure to organize and interpret our experiences.[3] This means that for young learners, exposure to stories enriches their mental models and allows them to interpret new information and experiences better.

Emotionally, children tend to identify with story characters and become personally invested in the plot. This can provoke a range of emotional reactions, which can help promote social and emotional growth.[4]

In the context of language learning, storytelling provides comprehensible input, which is the perfect raw data for learning.[5] This meaningful and comprehensible input promotes language acquisition, as students learn language from the data.

The overall result? Stories are incredibly effective at helping learners learn. Often more so than 'standard' ways of teaching, stories can affect cognitive, emotional and language development. It's not an exaggeration to say that storytelling can positively impact every aspect of language learning.

But this is just the tip of the iceberg. Let's look in more detail at each skill that stories can benefit.

Language Skills

Vocabulary

One of the biggest hurdles your students face is the sheer volume of new vocabulary. It's one of the most challenging things about language learning. So it's good news that one New Zealand study examined how effective reading stories aloud was for vocabulary acquisition in elementary school children.[6]

The results showed that story reading can be a significant source of vocabulary acquisition, and follow-up tests showed that this incidental vocabulary learning was relatively permanent. Even better, low-scoring children gained as much as high-scoring children.

Grammar

Grammar can be a daunting aspect of language learning. This is a shame, as a study showed a positive difference in grammar scores and students' beliefs towards using literary texts in language teaching. Another study mirrored these results after using short stories to see their effect on tested grammar scores.[7]

Hearing or seeing grammar structures used naturally in stories helps them acquire those rules 'naturally' or implicitly, without explicit learning. Our brains are pattern recognition machines, so they'll pick up the correct way to use grammar instinctively, even if students can't always articulate why - the same way we learn our first language.

As students listen to or read stories over time, they'll understand how different grammatical structures function in context. As they progress, they'll notice subtle distinctions in meaning based on speakers' grammatical choices. They can then replicate these structures in their own speech.

Pronunciation

Listening to native-level speakers tell stories is an excellent way for your students to improve their pronunciation and intonation. Encourage them to listen closely and mimic the storyteller's tone, pacing, and rhythm. As they practice, they'll gain greater control over their speech and develop a more natural-sounding accent in the target language.

Incredibly, even without specific mimicking practice, pronunciation can still improve. One study investigated how pronunciation was affected by listening to audio stories, and the learners showed a significant improvement in pronunciation proficiency compared to groups that hadn't listened to stories.[8]

Listening

As you would expect, listening to stories improves listening skills. A study investigated the impact of a systematic, story-reading-aloud program on the listening comprehension skills of young children.[9] The study involved 222 preschool and first-grade children randomly assigned to either a home- or school-based experimental group and was carried out by parents or teachers.

The author evaluated the effects on the children's listening comprehension skills, including their understanding of syntactic structures and story comprehension. The results were impressive, showing that preschool and first-grade children significantly improved their listening comprehension skills, regardless of whether at home or school.

Reading

Just as listening comprehension improves through practice, so time spent reading stories improves reading comprehension. Encourage your students to read stories that interest them, as this will increase their engagement and motivation.

One study that looked at this tested a reading program based on high-interest illustrated story books.[10] The study provided 380 Fijian pupils with 250 English storybooks and compared their progress to a control group who followed a traditional English language program. After eight months, pupils exposed to the story books progressed in reading and listening comprehension at twice the average rate, confirming the hypothesis that high-interest story reading has a vital role in second language learning. After 20 months, the gains had increased further and spread to related language skills.

Writing

One study examined the effects of using short stories to improve foreign language writing skills.[11] It was conducted over thirteen weeks in a primary school and aimed to investigate if there was a significant difference in the writing achievements of students who read more stories. The result? A positive effect on students' short story writing skills in terms of language, content, organization, and communicative achievement. Writing exercises will reinforce vocabulary and grammar skills and encourage creativity and self-expression.

Speaking

Even though you might think of reading and speaking as opposites - one is receptive and textual, the other producing and vocal - it makes sense that reading can help speaking. Again, as the brain is a pattern recognition machine, it absorbs and stores chunks and patterns for use later. It should come as no surprise that a study that investigated the effectiveness of using English short stories as material to develop students' speaking skills. It also helped students improve their spoken fluency, as well as develop an interest in reading generally.

Cognitive Skills

Motivation

Reading stories is seen as one of the most motivating activities in learning.[12] Often language learning can get a bad reputation as it's such a long journey. So, weaving storytelling into your lessons can make the process more enjoyable and engaging. As students delve into captivating narratives, they'll be motivated to learn and more likely to continue progressing. Compare the excitement of exploring stories to the monotony of vocabulary lists and grammar drills, and it's clear which method will keep students enthusiastic about learning.

Confidence

Incorporate group storytelling activities to create a low-pressure environment where students can practice their listening and speaking skills. By using stories they already know in their first language, students can leverage this knowledge to retell the stories in their target language. These collaborative activities will help build their confidence and encourage language produc-tion.[13]

Focus

Unsurprisingly, students pay more attention to stories than traditional educational formats like lectures or teacher-centred lessons. At least more so than reading out of a generic coursebook! A well-told story can capture their imagination and hold their interest, fostering a deeper engagement with the material and improving their focus and attention.

Creativity

Stories stretch students' creative muscles and stimulate their imaginations. Listening to and creating their own stories will inspire them to take risks and think outside the box, leading to a more vibrant and dynamic learning experience. One study showed that storytelling could expand the creative potential of schoolchildren across a wide range of tasks.[14]

Memory

Our brains seem to be wired to remember stories. Research has shown that information presented in a story format is more likely to be retained than information presented straightforwardly. A study by Paul Nation showed the dangers of learning vocabulary in lexical sets (i.e. grouping by topic).[15] You can help your students commit new language concepts to memory more effectively by tapping into this innate affinity for narrative, where new lexical items are presented in context and in a more authentic way.

Critical thinking

Encourage your students to analyze and interpret the stories they hear to improve their critical thinking skills. By providing well-prepared tasks and guiding them through the process, you'll help them think more deeply about the world around them and become more discerning learners.

Stress-reduction

Stories can provide a soothing escape from everyday worries, allowing students to immerse themselves in different worlds and reduce feelings of stress and anxiety. Incorporating storytelling into your language classroom will create a more relaxed and supportive learning environment.

Rapport

From a teacher's point of view, storytelling can help you build rapport with your students by allowing you to connect on a more personal level. Sharing and discussing stories will create a positive and supportive classroom environment, helping your students feel more comfortable and confident in their language learning journey.

Culture

One of the most significant benefits of using stories in language education is the cultural understanding your students can gain. This understanding will enhance their language skills and enable them to communicate more effectively with native speakers. By introducing them to the stories and traditions of different cultures, you'll help them develop a deeper appreciation of those cultures and their values.

Collaboration

Use stories as a focal point for teamwork, encouraging students to collaborate on activities like acting out scenes or discussing narratives as a group. Incorporate group activities into your lessons, where students can share their own stories, discuss those they've read or listened to, and offer feedback to their peers. This collaborative approach strengthens their language skills and builds community within the classroom.

In Summary

Stories can be used for all age groups and greatly benefit language teachers and students.

- Some of these benefits are improved vocabulary acquisition, listening and reading comprehension, grammar acquisition, fluency, writing skills, and pronunciation.
- Stories can also improve cognitive skills such as motivation, confidence, focus, creativity, memory, critical thinking, stress reduction, rapport-building, and collaboration.
- Using stories can help students develop cultural understanding and connect with others through collaborative activities.

There are so many benefits that the question becomes, why wouldn't we use stories more often in our teaching?

II

Stories & Storytelling

4

Preparation

So you're convinced that stories are a wonderful tool for your classes. Great!

But what exactly is a story? And where do you find suitable stories for your students? And then how do you then prepare a story for your class?

This section will dive into the world of storytelling and explore the various elements that make up a great story. We'll pull apart what a story is, the component parts of a story and how to find or create a great one. Using examples, we'll then look at how to prepare it for your language lessons.

Finally, in section IV, we'll look at the activities you can use with those stories.

Let's go!

5

Where to Find Stories

Stories are everywhere.

They're all around us – movies, books, podcasts, conversations with friends – stories are woven into the fabric of our lives. With a little bit of practice, you'll be plucking them out of everyday occurrences with ease. Until then, you can borrow stories from other sources with no issue.

To get you started, here are some of the most common categories of stories you can use in your lessons.

Folktales

Folktales are windows into the soul of a culture. They're timeless stories passed down through generations, often imparting moral lessons through narratives set in mystical worlds, featuring magical creatures and extraordinary events. Delve into folktales, and you'll discover an endless supply of stories to spark the imagination.

Fables

Fables are where morality meets the animal kingdom. They're short, engaging tales that teach moral lessons, and usually feature animals as the main characters. These digestible tales are perfect for introducing bite-sized lessons (and new language structures and lexis!)

Myths

Myths are explorations of beliefs and customs. They're fascinating stories that uncover the beliefs and customs of a culture, and often feature gods, goddesses, and other supernatural beings. Introducing myths to your students offers a window into human beliefs and values from around the world.

Legends

Legends are history, myth and folklore combined. They're stories rooted in historical events, although often mixed with elements of myth and folklore. You can transport your students to bygone eras, introducing them to historical figures and events that have shaped our world. And don't forget to explore the realm of modern 'urban legends' as well!

Personal anecdotes

These are tales from your own life experiences. I'm sure your life is a treasure trove of unique, authentic stories (and, if you're like me, some rather embarrassing ones). Sharing personal anecdotes can help students connect with the target language culture while building rapport. If you borrow stories from friends, colleagues and family, respect their privacy and remove identifiable information.

Students' anecdotes

Encouraging students to share personal anecdotes can enhance language skills and create a supportive learning environment. Students can develop their speaking, listening, and writing skills through the powerful medium of their own stories. Remember to approach this sensitively, respect them and their culture, and never insist students share their personal stories.

Current events

News and current affairs offer endless stories that you can adapt to your students' interests and language levels. You can teach language concepts, cultural knowledge, and critical thinking skills while keeping your students engaged and informed.

Adapt a story

What if you can't find the perfect story? Or what if you love a particular story but don't think it fits your students well?

Remember that if nothing quite fits (or if you don't have time to search on the internet for hours!) You can create your own stories or adapt one you know, quickly and easily.

To do that, you must know the common elements of stories and story frameworks. Most stories have an underlying framework that they follow.

6

Story Elements

Think of stories as a set of building blocks, like Lego. You can use pieces in different ways to build something new. There are some elements that every good story has, and knowing what these are can help you when you're creating or adapting stories. Here they are!

Characters

These are the people, creatures, or objects populating the story and driving the action. Characters include the protagonist (the hero), antagonist (the villain), plus supporting and minor characters. Creating relatable and intriguing characters can capture students' attention and build an emotional connection with the story.

Setting

The setting is the time and place where the story occurs. A good setting gives context, atmosphere, and cultural information. A great setting will immerse students in different environments and customs while they absorb new language.

Plot

The plot is the series of events that make up the story and propel the action. A well-crafted plot can help convey key lessons while keeping students engaged and eager to know what happens next.

Conflict

Conflict is the problem or challenge(s) the hero must overcome. It can be external, between the hero and another character or force, or internal, within the hero themselves. Introducing conflicts in your story can create suspense, pique students' curiosity, and encourage them to think critically.

Theme

The theme is the underlying message or idea expressed in the story. It can address topics like love, courage, friendship, or any other significant aspect of life. Incorporating themes into your stories can prompt students to reflect on essential life lessons and connect language learning with real-life experiences.

Point of view

This is the perspective from which the story is told. The point of view can be first person, second person, or third person. Each of these will have an enormous effect on how your students will perceive the story. Experimenting with different points of view can provide fresh perspectives and encourage students to explore various ways of storytelling (especially for more advanced learners).

Tone

The tone is the mood or atmosphere of the story. It can be serious, lighthearted, suspenseful or heartwarming – or any other emotion. Adjusting the tone can create emotional variety, ensuring that stories resonate with students on different levels.

Symbolism

Symbolism uses symbols to represent ideas, emotions, or other story elements. Incorporating symbolism can add depth and meaning, stimulating students' analytical thinking and enhancing their understanding of complex concepts.

By understanding and incorporating these essential story elements, language teachers can create a captivating and memorable learning experience for their students. So, go ahead and play with these building blocks to weave your tales, making language learning an enchanting journey for your students.

Not sure how to fit these and the frameworks together? Example coming right up.

Applying the Elements

Let's use the story of a teacher who broke their toe on the way to school but continued to teach their classes anyway to see how all of these fit together.

- **Title:** The Hurried Teacher
- **Characters:** The teacher, the protagonist
- **Setting:** On the way to school
- **Plot:** The teacher is in a hurry to get to school and is not paying attention to where they are going. They trip and fall, breaking their toe in the process. Despite the pain, the teacher continues on to school, determined to make it on time for their students.

- **Conflict:** The conflict in the story is the teacher's injury, and the challenge of getting to school on time despite the pain.
- **Theme:** The story's theme is the importance of determination and perseverance, even facing obstacles.
- **Point of View:** The point of view is first person, as the teacher is the protagonist and the person telling the story.
- **Tone:** The story's tone is serious but also determined, as the teacher is determined to make it to school despite their injury.
- **Symbolism:** The broken toe symbolises overcoming obstacles and the importance of perseverance.

This short anecdote demonstrates how the common elements of stories can be incorporated into a brief and engaging story. By using elements such as characters, setting, plot, conflict, theme, point of view, tone, and symbolism, language teachers can create memorable and compelling stories for language learning.

The teacher's personal story can inspire and motivate your students and demonstrate the importance of determination and perseverance.

Not all stories are lengthy – as we've looked at, some are short, personal anecdotes that may only be a few sentences. While some of the above will apply, simplicity is the key here.

7

Story Frameworks

Whatever your story, you can probably make it better by using a story framework.

A story framework is like a colour-by-numbers template. While the template (the framework) remains the same, it can be copied and coloured differently each time a story is created. We'll look at six different templates we can use to create stories (you can also use frameworks to see if there are any gaps in your story!).

Let's continue to use the anecdote of a teacher who broke their toe.

The Three-Act Structure

The three-act structure is used in countless stories. Everyone from Shakespeare to modern superhero movies makes use of it. There's a good reason for this - the three-act structure works well with dramatic stories of good and evil, or conflict and resolution.

This structure divides a story into three parts called 'acts': setup, confrontation, and resolution. It's a classic formula that unfolds like this:

- *Act 1 – Setup:* Our intrepid teacher dashes to school, racing against the clock.
- *Act 2 – Confrontation:* The teacher trips, breaking their toe, but refuses to give up.
- *Act 3 – Resolution:* The teacher, fueled by determination, reaches school on time, overcoming their painful obstacle, and teaches a fantastic lesson.

Although it might not seem like Act 2 is a confrontation against a person, it's a confrontation against the teacher's inner demons - the voices telling him to give up and go home. The teacher confronts those and makes a hard choice, before winning and continuing the journey.

The Hero's Journey

The Hero's Journey follows the hero through a series of stages, as if the story were a journey. Each is given a name, and this structure transforms our tale into an epic saga:

- *Call to Adventure:* Our teacher is summoned to the school, driven by their duty to their students.
- *Road of Trials:* The teacher faces the challenge of a broken toe, yet courageously presses on.
- *Return to the Ordinary World:* The triumphant teacher arrives at school, having conquered their ordeal and fulfilled their mission.

The full version of the 'Hero's Journey' framework, created by Joseph Campbell[16], has seventeen sections, but these three are enough for us to plan a lesson activity.

The Linear Structure

The linear structure framework presents events in a simple, linear progression from beginning to end, making the story easy to follow and digest:

The teacher hurries to school, stumbles and breaks their toe, but overcomes the pain and arrives on time, teaching their students against all odds.

The Non-Linear Structure

The non-linear structure framework weaves together events in a non-chronological order, challenging students to piece together the tale's puzzle:

The teacher arrives at school despite their broken toe. The story then rewinds, revealing the teacher's fall and their unwavering determination to press on, despite the painful obstacle.

The Cycle Structure

The cycle structure framework has events that recur in a cyclical pattern, highlighting themes and character development:

Our teacher faces numerous obstacles on their way to school but perseveres, exemplifying determination and resilience. The cycle repeats as the teacher continues to conquer challenges, teaching the invaluable lesson of perseverance in both language learning and life.

Using the Frameworks

By harnessing the power of different story frameworks, you can breathe new life into even the simplest anecdote, transforming it into an unforgettable tale that will captivate your students. Experiment with various frameworks to emphasize different themes or ideas, creating a magical storytelling experience that will keep your students spellbound.

Remember, any story you want to use in your lesson, mentally run it through one of these frameworks to check that it meets the criteria.

- Does it make sense?
- Do any parts need to be filled in or expanded, or shortened?
- Which framework is the most suitable?
- Would it have a greater impact if it had a different structure?
- Does it meet all the points of your chosen structure?

III

Stories & Lesson Planning

8

A Story-Planning Method

When preparing a story for a lesson, I use a process, a checklist, of things to prepare.

I call this the 'Story-Planning Method' and will share it with you now. As with all good lesson plans, it starts with the lesson aim.

Aim

What's the aim of your lesson? What are the language goals? Are there any other goals? What vocabulary or grammar structures do you want to teach your students?

Choose a story that aligns with your language goals and will help your students achieve those goals.

Ensure that the story you choose is appropriate for their language proficiency and that it won't be too difficult for them to understand.

If the story is too challenging, your students may become frustrated and lose interest, so choosing a story that is just right for their level is essential.

- Will they be practising a skill like listening, reading
- Will you need to pre-teach any vocabulary?
- Will you need to plan for more repetition of tricky words or phrases?

Story

Which story are you going to use? See Chapter 5 for ideas on where to find stories. Your students are more likely to be engaged in the story if they can relate to it or find it interesting. So, consider your students' interests and choose appropriately. It could be a story about a topic they're passionate about, a story set in a location they're interested in, or a story featuring characters they can relate to.

Finally, consider the length of the story. If you have limited time, choose a short story you can finish in one lesson. If you have more time, you can select a longer story and divide it into several classes. Here are some ways to avoid common mistakes:

Incorporate interesting elements

Once you have a better understanding of your students' interests, you can start incorporating elements of those interests into the story. For example, if your students are interested in sports, you could choose a story that features a sports theme or takes place in a sporting venue. If your students are interested in music, you could choose a story that features a musical performance or a musician.

Use relatable characters

Another way to personalise a story is by using characters your students can relate to. For example, you could choose a story with characters similar in age, gender, or background to your students. This can help your students connect with the story and feel more invested.

Encourage student contributions

Finally, you can personalise a story by allowing your students to contribute. For example, you could ask your students to suggest characters or events they want to see in the story. You could brainstorm and change characters on the fly, or take suggestions for the next lesson.

Format

How will you present the story to your students? First, decide which skill you want to practice – listening, reading, or both. Then choose a format that matches this skill. The good news is, you have lots of options.

If you want to practise listening comprehension

- Tell aloud - Tell the story yourself, out loud (and perhaps while sitting in a circle?)
- Play a recording of the story, or use a podcast format
- Students tell aloud - ask students to tell the story to each other
- Video - play a video of the story

If you want to practise reading comprehension

- Ask students to read individually
- A pairwork reading activity (each student has different information)
- Split the story into parts and put them up on the walls of the classroom

It's nice (but not essential) to have a reason for your choice that you can tell your students. You can include this reason in your context – even a silly one. For example, you were writing a story, and 'your dog ate your story,' so it's now in several pieces, and you hope your students can help you put it back together again.

Materials

I view materials are anything you want to use in a lesson to support learning that you'll need to prepare beforehand. You should ensure that your materials are relevant, and support your lesson aims.

As the saying goes, keep things as simple as possible but no simpler. Don't use extra materials unnecessarily, but make sure you have those you need to support students in the tasks.

Materials should be:

1. Engaging – they need to keep your learners' attention!
2. A language model – they need to target the correct language.
3. Supportive – they should support weaker learners.
4. Exploitable – ideally, you can use them more than once in a lesson.
5. Natural – considering student levels, they'll be as close to authentic language use as possible.

For more information on this, my book 'Lesson Planning for Language Teachers'[17] goes into much more depth on this subject.

Don't forget about props and music! You can use props such as pictures, costumes, props, puppets or flashcards to help students visualise the story. Done well, these can make the story way more fun, keep learners focused and improve their understanding.

Group Dynamics

How will you group your students for the activities? Interaction patterns describe the number of students working together. Usually, we talk about:

- Individual work (students work on their own).

- Pair work (two students work together).
- Small group work (3-5 students).
- Large group work (5+ students).
- Whole class (everyone together).

It's a good idea to have a mix of these patterns in a lesson. Too much of one interaction pattern and the lesson can be repetitive. Too many changes can distract from the lesson content.

How should you choose which grouping to use for which activity?

A rule of thumb is that if you want to focus on form, use the larger groupings and whole class first, rather than pick on individuals (and putting them under a lot of pressure with a possibility of losing face if they get the answer wrong).

If you ask students to be creative, go with the smaller groupings and individual work. This allows everyone to have a try at creating, rather than some people's work being swallowed up by stronger personalities.

9

One-Page Planning Summary

To plan to use a story in your lesson, ask yourself these questions one by one:

Aim: What are the aims of your lesson? What are the language points and/or skills you'd like to teach or practice?

Story: Which story are you going to use? How is it personalised for your students?

Format: How will you present the story? Make sure it aligns with any skill practice in your aim.

Materials: How much support will they need with the language and skill they'll be using? Do you need to adapt the story's language?

Activity: What task or activity will you do with your students?

Group dynamics: How will you group your students for the activities?

10

Storytelling Techniques

OK, so the lesson has started, and you're ready to begin.

Here are a few pointers to warm your students up and some techniques to enhance the storytelling experience.

Pre-story

It's 'follow–your–plan' time!

Before telling the story, you can do several things to help your students prepare for the lesson:

Set the context

Before the story, you can set the context by providing background information about the story, setting, and characters. This helps prepare the students to understand the story better and get more involved in the lesson.

Pre-teach vocabulary

You can pre-teach language related to the story. This helps students understand the story more quickly and also helps improve their vocabulary. Some simple activities that students can do individually or in small groups could be:

- **Word Match:** match words related to the story with their definitions.
- **Word Jumble:** unscramble words linked to the story.
- **Picture Match:** match story pictures to their descriptions.

Engage your students

You can use various techniques to get students excited about the story. For example, they can ask questions to generate interest, provide a brief story overview, or use props or visual aids to capture their attention.

Encourage students to make connections

Ask students questions to help them connect the story with their own lives. Ask if they know a similar person, place, or event. This makes the lesson more relevant to their own experiences, which builds connections and helps them remember it better.

Encourage participation

You can encourage students to participate in the story by asking questions, encouraging them to make predictions, or asking them to act out parts of the story. This helps students get more involved in the lesson and improves their language skills.

Get your props ready

You can use props such as pictures, costumes, or props to help students visualise the story. This makes the story more engaging and allows students to understand it better.

Choose the storytelling space

Designate a space for storytelling. This indicates to students that it's story time, and helps them get into the right frame of mind. Sitting in a circle or semi-circle is great, if possible.

During the story

It's story time!

As you tell the story, keep a close eye on your students and consider the support they might need. Monitor how the story connects with them and how you might need to alter the delivery. Look through these tips, but if you're new to storytelling, don't try implementing all these at once! Take your time and play around with these over time.

Use your props

Using props and visual aids can make stories come to life and make them more engaging for your students. For example, you could use puppets, masks, or flashcards to help illustrate the story and make it more memorable for your students.

Encourage participation

Encouraging student participation is a great way to make stories more interactive and engaging. You could ask your students to act out parts of the story, contribute ideas for characters or events, or make predictions about what will happen next.

Use music and sound effects

Adding music and sound effects to your stories can make them more immersive and help create a memorable learning experience. You could use background music, sound effects, or even student-created sound effects to help bring the story to life.

Use technology

You could use technology to make your stories more engaging and interactive. For example, you could use digital storytelling tools, multimedia presentations, or augmented reality to help bring the story to life and make it more memorable for your students.

Pacing

Varying the story's pace can help keep students interested and engaged. You can slow down during essential parts of the story to build suspense or speed up during less important parts to keep the story moving (you can alter the playback speed in a recording as well!)

Tone

Using different tones of voice can help to bring the story to life and make it more memorable. For example, using a high-pitched voice for a child character or a deep voice for a villain can help students better understand and visualise the characters.

Body Language

Using gestures, facial expressions, and other forms of body language can help to bring the story to life and make it more memorable. For example, using hand gestures to show movement or facial expressions to show emotions can help students better understand the story.

Visual Aids

Using props, pictures, or other visual aids can help to bring the story to life and make it more memorable. For example, using a picture of a character to help students visualise the story or using props to show objects in the story can help students to understand the story better.

Repetition

Repeating the story's key parts can help students better understand and remember the story. For example, repeating important phrases or events can help students understand and remember the story better.

So, folks, as you can see, there are many techniques that you can use to make stories more engaging and interactive. By incorporating these techniques into your storytelling-based language lessons, you can help your students develop a deeper connection to the language and culture and make language learning more enjoyable and effective.

11

Assessment with Stories

One of our primary goals is to create a learning environment where students can acquire new language skills.

Imagine entering a vibrant, engaging classroom where students eagerly share stories from various cultures, explore new worlds, and learn. However, ensuring that each student progresses and benefits from these storytelling activities can be challenging without an effective assessment system.

Assessing students through storytelling allows you to monitor their development, provide valuable feedback, and adapt your teaching strategies to meet their individual needs.

There are two types of assessment we can use for this: formative and summative assessment.

Formative assessment focuses on monitoring progress and providing feedback during learning, helping students fine-tune their skills and grow as language learners. Think of it as a GPS that guides students, step by step, towards their language learning goals.

On the other hand, summative assessment evaluates the overall language proficiency of your students through storytelling tasks and projects. It offers a snapshot of their achievements at a specific point in time, like a final destination on a map.

45

Using these can create a comprehensive and balanced approach to measuring language proficiency and skill development.

12

Formative Assessment

Formative assessment is an ongoing process that involves monitoring students' progress, identifying areas for improvement, and providing feedback.

So what does this mean, in practical terms? What would should you be doing as a teacher to assess formatively? Here are some easy techniques that you can start doing straight away.

Observation and anecdotal records

As you listen to students share stories or participate in storytelling activities, note their language use - things they're doing well and things that are challenging them. Jot down specific examples that highlight their strengths and areas for improvement. These anecdotal records can help you tailor your teaching approach and provide targeted feedback.

Another way to do this is to create mini-rubrics that you can use in class. These might take the form of 'can-do' statements. 'Can use the past simple tense correctly' might be one. You'd have a list that relates to the lesson alongside a list of student names. Then, when you catch a student performing well and achieving one, tick it off (and remember to give some praise!).

Questioning and discussion techniques

Encourage students to think critically and express their thoughts by asking open-ended questions related to the story, such as "How do you think the main character feels?" or "What do you think the author wants us to learn from this story?" By analysing their responses, you can assess their comprehension, vocabulary, and communication skills.

Story retelling and summarizing activities

Ask students to retell a story in their own words, either orally or in writing. This exercise not only checks their comprehension but also allows you to evaluate their language skills, such as grammar, vocabulary, and sentence structure. Additionally, summarizing activities can help students practice identifying the main ideas and important details of a story.

Peer and self-assessment

Invite students to evaluate their own or their classmates' storytelling performances using pre-established criteria or rubrics. This collaborative process not only enhances their critical thinking skills but also fosters a sense of ownership over their learning.

Progress journals or portfolios

Encourage students to maintain a journal or portfolio where they can document their storytelling experiences, reflect on their progress, and set personal goals. Reviewing these journals can give you a better understanding of each student's learning journey and help you provide meaningful feedback.

Remember to give feedback

When offering feedback, be specific, constructive, and focus on areas where the student can improve. For example, instead of saying "Your storytelling needs work," you might say, "Your story was engaging, but try to use more varied sentence structures to make it even more captivating."

Focusing on specific language skills

Target your feedback on the particular language skills your students are working on, such as pronunciation, grammar, or vocabulary. Doing so, you help them understand where they need to focus their efforts and what strategies to use for improvement.

Balancing praise and criticism

Remember to acknowledge your students' successes and efforts while pointing out areas for improvement. A balanced approach to feedback can boost their confidence and motivate them to continue striving for growth.

Individualized and targeted feedback

Take the time to provide personalized feedback that addresses each student's unique needs and learning style. By doing so, you demonstrate your commitment to their progress.

13

Summative Assessment

Summative assessment evaluates students at the end of a unit, course, or specific period. These assessments provide a snapshot of students' achievements and can inform future instructional decisions, grading, or reporting.

Most schools have some kind of end-of-unit or end-of-course test already in place. In addition to that, here are some practical ideas for how to start assessing summatively.

Written or oral storytelling tasks

Narrative essays: Invite students to write a well-structured narrative essay based on a given prompt, theme or set of guidelines. This task allows you to assess their writing skills, creativity, and understanding of storytelling elements.

Oral presentations: Have students prepare and deliver an oral storytelling performance, either individually or in groups. Through this activity, you can evaluate their speaking, listening, and presentation skills and their ability to engage an audience.

Digital storytelling projects: Encourage students to create digital stories using multimedia tools such as videos, podcasts, or slide presentations. This innovative approach showcases their language skills and demonstrates their digital literacy and creativity.

Story analysis and interpretation

Comprehension quizzes or tests: Design quizzes or tests that assess students' understanding of key story elements, themes, and vocabulary. These assessments can take various forms, such as multiple-choice, short-answer, or matching questions.

Critical analysis essays or presentations: Ask students to analyze a story in depth, exploring themes, characters, or literary techniques. This task enables you to assess their critical thinking, writing, and communication skills and their ability to interpret and analyze stories.

Creative extension activities

Creating original stories: Challenge students to craft original stories, incorporating specific language features, themes, or storytelling techniques. This activity allows you to evaluate their creativity, writing skills, and understanding of storytelling principles.

Adapting stories into different formats (e.g., plays, comics): Encourage students to transform a story into a different format, such as a play, comic, or animated video. This creative task showcases their understanding of story structure, adaptation, and ability to work with different media.

Developing assessment rubrics

Ensure that your assessment rubrics reflect the learning objectives of your storytelling unit, focusing on specific language skills, content knowledge, and critical thinking abilities.

Design your rubrics to capture students' proficiency in various language skills, offering a comprehensive and holistic evaluation of their language development. Besides language skills, consider assessing students' creativity, problem-solving, and critical thinking abilities, essential components of compelling storytelling.

By employing diverse assessment techniques and developing clear, objective rubrics, you can create a meaningful and engaging assessment experience for your students.

14

Balancing Assessment

The best way to know how your students are doing is to balance formative and summative assessments.

The great thing about these two assessment methods is their complementary roles. Consider formative assessment as a guiding role, micro-correcting students before they get too far off course. Summative assessment is more a showcase of the best that they can do.

It's also useful to adapt assessments for different learners. You'll find students with diverse backgrounds, abilities, and needs in any classroom. You can create an inclusive and supportive learning environment by adapting your assessment approaches to suit these differences. For instance, you might offer alternative assessment formats, provide additional scaffolding or support, or adjust assessment criteria to accommodate different skill levels.

Finally, it's good to reflect on your assessment procedures occasionally. Regularly review your assessment strategies, considering feedback from students, colleagues, or observations. By embracing continuous improvement, you can ensure that your assessment practices remain relevant, engaging, and aligned with the evolving needs of your students.

IV

Story Activities

15

How to Use Activities

So far, you've read a lot of theory – now it's time for practice! I'd strongly suggest you don't use several of these simultaneously in a lesson. Instead, follow a process like this:

1. Choose and prepare your story (sections II and III)
2. Identify the target language you want to focus on in the story.
3. Review storytelling techniques (section IV)
4. Decide how you're going to assess your students (section V)
5. Browse through this section and choose an activity that appeals to you.
6. Visualise the process of how the activity will run with your story.
7. Consider if you'll need to adapt any part of the activity based on your learners.
8. Incorporate the story into your lesson plan.
9. Teach, and after the lesson, take two minutes to jot down notes on what went well and what to try next time.

Some of the activities mention awarding points – this is useful for young learners and some adult classes, but be aware that some classes might find this demotivating. Also, extension and alternative activities listed can often be used as homework. Good luck, and have fun!

16

Comic Strip Story

Preparation

1. Prepare blank comic strip templates, or find pre-made templates online.

Materials

- Blank comic strip templates, pencils, and markers.

Activity

1. Introduce the story and its characters, using the target language frequently.
2. Divide the class into small groups, each assigned a different part of the story.
3. Explain to the students that they will create a comic strip to retell their part of the story, using as much of the target language as possible.
4. Give each group a blank comic strip template and pencils or markers.
5. Allow the groups time to plan and draw their comic strips, emphasizing the use of the target language in their dialogue and narration.
6. Let each group share their comic strip with the class, retelling their part

of the story using the target language.

Extension

- Ask the students to write a new ending to the story and illustrate it in a new comic strip.
- Have the students work in pairs or small groups to retell the entire story in comic strip format, using as much of the target language as possible.

Alternatives

- Instead of assigning different parts of the story to each group, you could provide the students with comic strip templates and ask them to create their own story, using the target language.
- You could ask the students to create a dialogue-only comic strip.

17

Diorama

Preparation

1. Prepare materials for making dioramas.

Materials

- Shoeboxes, construction paper, scissors, glue, and any other materials students may want to use to create their dioramas.

Activity

1. Explain to the students that they will create a diorama related to the story.
2. Provide the students with materials for making dioramas. Ask them to plan and create their diorama based on a key scene or location in the story.
3. Allow the students to work on their dioramas, providing support and guidance as needed.

Extension

- Ask the students to write a new scene to the story and create a new diorama related to the scene.
- Have the students work in pairs or small groups to retell the story in their own words, using as much of the target language as possible.

Alternatives

- Instead of creating a diorama, you could ask the students to create a puppet show related to the story.
- You could ask the students to create their own dioramas or puppet shows related to the story or a new scene.

18

Family Stories

Preparation

1. Ask the students to talk to their families and collect stories related to their family history, traditions, or culture.
2. Provide the students with a list of interview questions that will help them collect stories and information related to their family history.
3. Be aware of the cultural sensitivity and privacy of the family members. Also be sensitive to students with missing family members or unusual circumstances.

Materials

- Audio or video recording equipment to capture the interviews.
- A list of interview questions.

1. Introduce the activity to the class, emphasizing the importance of family stories and their cultural significance.
2. Provide the students with a list of interview questions and brief them on

the interviewing process.

3. Have the students collect stories from their family members,.
4. Once the interviews are complete, have the students share their findings with the class,.
5. Encourage the students to compare and contrast their findings.

Extension

- Ask the students to create a written or oral presentation of their findings,.
- Have the students create illustrations or animations to accompany their retelling of the stories,.

Alternatives

- You could ask the students to create a family tree or map,.
- You could ask the students to create a written or oral reflection on the importance of family stories and their cultural significance,.

Assessment

- Observe how often the students use the target language in their interviews and storytelling.
- Make notes on their pronunciation, vocabulary use, and grammar in their contributions.

19

Flip Book

Preparation

1. Prepare materials for making flipbooks, such as paper, scissors, and markers.

Materials

- Students may want to use paper, scissors, markers, and any other materials to create their flipbooks.

Activity

1. Explain to the students that they will create a flip book related to the story, emphasizing the target language.
2. Provide the students with materials for making flip books, and ask them to work in pairs to plan and create their flip book based on a key scene or location in the story.
3. Allow the students to work on their flip books, providing support and guidance as needed, and
4. Let the students share their flip books with another pair and take turns

to flip through them to tell their story.

Extension

- Ask the students to write a new scene to the story and create a new flipbook related to the scene, emphasizing the target language.
- Have the students work in pairs or small groups to retell the story in their own words, using as much of the target language as possible.

Alternatives

- Instead of creating a flip book, you could ask the students to create a comic strip related to the story.
- You could ask the students to create their own flip books or comic strips related to the story or a new scene.

20

Forgetful Storyteller

Preparation

1. None needed.

Materials

- None needed.

Activity

1. Begin telling the story to the class, but act as if you keep forgetting the details.
2. Every time you forget a detail, ask a different student to fill in the blank.
3. After each student has contributed to the story, recap what has been added so far.
4. Continue telling the story, "forgetting" details and soliciting help from different students, until the story is complete.
5. Have the class discuss what they liked and what could be improved about the story.

Extension

- Ask the students to work in pairs or small groups to retell the story from memory.
- Have the students create a new ending or a sequel to the story.

Alternatives

- You could ask the students to create a new story in the same "forgetful" format, with each student taking turns as the forgetful storyteller.
- You could ask the students to work in pairs or small groups to create a story together, but each student can only add one sentence at a time.

21

Improv Story

Preparation

1. Prepare a list of prompts or sentence starters related to the story.

Materials

- Sentence starters

Activity

1. Introduce the story and its characters, using the target language frequently.
2. Explain to the students that they will improvise a new version of the story, using prompts or sentence starters.
3. Divide the class into small groups, each focusing on a different part of the story.
4. Give each group a prompt or sentence starter related to their part of the story, and let them improvise the next part of the story using the target language.
5. Allow each group to perform their improvisation for the class, using

props or costumes to help bring the story to life.

6. Encourage students to use the target language as much as possible, to help them develop their language skills.

Extensions

- Ask the students to write their own version of the story, using the target language to describe their own creative ideas and interpretations.
- Have the students work in pairs or small groups to retell the story in their own words, using as much of the target language as possible.

Alternatives

- Instead of using prompts or sentence starters, you could provide the students with pictures and ask them to improvise a story based on the pictures.
- You could ask the students to create their own sentence starters or prompts to share with the class.

22

Jigsaw Story

Preparation

1. Before the lesson, divide your chosen stories into segments or pieces, like a jigsaw puzzle.
2. You could do this with a written story, use pictures of scenes, or even use an image of a key person or object to represent a scene.

Materials

- Jigsaw story, one copy for each group

Activity

1. Group students into pairs or small groups
2. Give each group a set of puzzle pieces.
3. Each group must assemble the puzzle pieces in the correct order to complete the story.
4. Students then tell the story aloud and/or write down the full story. Ask students to use the target language as often as possible with natural language.

Extension

- Groups switch written stories and try and find errors.

Alternatives

Use more than one story to create a jigsaw. Students take turns telling each other their story. Then, when students finish their story, split the group and pair with a student with a different story.

23

Mad Libs

Preparation

1. Create a short story, but leave out some key words, such as nouns, verbs, adjectives, and adverbs.
2. Create a list of options for each missing word.

Materials

- Copies of the story with missing words for each student.

Activity

1. Hand out the story with missing words to each student, and explain the "Mad Libs" concept, where each person fills in the blanks with the options provided.
2. Have the students work individually to fill in the missing words.
3. Once the students have filled in the missing words, have them read their completed story aloud to the class.
4. Have the class discuss what they liked and what could be improved about the stories.

Extension

- Ask the students to work in pairs or small groups to create their own Mad Libs story structure.
- Have the students create illustrations to accompany their story.

Alternatives

- You could ask the students to create a Mad Libs story using specific vocabulary or grammar structures.
- You could ask the students to create a Mad Libs story based on a specific topic, such as a favorite hobby or a memorable vacation.

24

Memory Game

Preparation

1. Create a list of related vocabulary words or phrases to the story, emphasizing the target language.

Materials

- Paper and pencils.
- Vocabulary list.

Activity

1. Explain to the students that they will play a memory game related to the story, emphasizing the target language.
2. Provide the students with a list of related vocabulary words or phrases to the story, emphasizing the use of the target language in their responses.
3. Allow the students to study the list of vocabulary words or phrases for a few minutes.
4. Ask the students to turn their papers over and try to write down as many vocabulary words or phrases as they can remember, emphasizing the use

of the target language in their responses.

5. Let the students compare their lists with a partner and discuss the words or phrases they remembered, emphasizing the use of the target language in their explanations and descriptions.

Extension

- Ask the students to write a new scene to the story and create a new list of related vocabulary words or phrases to the new scene, emphasizing the target language.
- Have the students work in pairs or small groups to retell the story in their own words, using as much of the target language as possible.

Alternatives

- Instead of providing a list of vocabulary words or phrases, you could give the students pictures or images related to the story and ask them to describe the images.
- You could ask the students to create their own memory games related to the story or a new scene.

25

Mind Mapping

Preparation

1. Prepare a list of related themes or topics to the story, emphasizing the target language.

Materials

- Paper and pencils.

Activity

1. Divide the class into small groups and explain that they will create a mind map related to the story, emphasizing the target language.
2. Provide each group with paper and pencils and encourage them to brainstorm related themes or topics to the story, emphasizing the use of the target language in their responses.
3. Allow the groups to create their mind maps, emphasizing the use of the target language in their organization and labelling.
4. Let each group share their mind maps with the class, emphasizing the

use of the target language in their explanations and descriptions.

5. Encourage the students to provide feedback on each other's work, focusing on language use and creativity.

Extension

- Ask the students to write a new scene to the story and create a mind map related to the new scene, emphasizing the target language in their organization and labeling.
- Have the students work in pairs or small groups to retell the story in their own words, using as much of the target language as possible.

Alternatives

- Instead of paper and pencils, you could provide the students with digital mind-mapping tools.
- You could ask the students to create their own mind maps based on different story prompts.

26

Modern Fairy Tales

Preparation

1. Choose a classic fairy tale that is familiar to the students.
2. Prepare materials for the activity, such as writing prompts, graphic organizers, and markers.

Materials

- Writing prompts, graphic organizers, markers, and any other materials students may want to use to create their modernized fairy tale.

Activity

1. Introduce the classic fairy tale and its characters.
2. Explain to the students that they will be modernizing the fairy tale.
3. Provide the students with writing prompts or graphic organizers to help them plan and organize their modernized fairy tale.
4. Allow the students to work on their modernized fairy tale, providing support and guidance as needed.

Extension

- Ask the students to create illustrations or animations to accompany their modernized fairy tale.
- Have the students work in pairs or small groups to create a modernized fairy tale script and perform it as a play.

Alternatives

- You could provide a list of potential fairy tales for the students to modernize.
- You could ask the students to create a modernized fairy tale in a different format, such as a comic strip or a video.

27

One-Word Story

Preparation

1. Introduce the concept of storytelling and its importance in language learning.
2. Provide examples of storytelling techniques, such as character development, plot development, and imagery.

Materials

- Writing materials, such as pens and paper.
- A list of storytelling techniques.

Activity

1. Explain the rules of the activity: each student will take turns to say one word until the story is complete.
2. Start the story with a simple sentence, such as "Once upon a time, there was a...".
3. Have the students take turns to say one word, focusing on the use of the target language in their contributions.

4. Encourage the students to use the list of storytelling techniques to create a well-developed story.
5. Once the story is complete, have the students read it aloud.
6. Encourage the students to compare and contrast the different contributions and their impact on the story.

Extension

- Ask the students to create illustrations or animations to accompany their story.
- Have the students present their story as a play or puppet show.

Alternatives

- You could ask the students to create a group story, emphasizing collaboration and teamwork in storytelling.

<h1 style="text-align:center">28</h1>

Personal Fables

Preparation

1. Introduce the concept of fables and their use of animal characters to represent people and their behaviors.
2. Provide examples of fables and their morals to the class.
3. Ask the students to think of a personal experience or story they would like to tell using animal characters to represent people.
4. Provide the students with a list of animal characters and their traits to help them create their fable.

Materials

- Writing materials, such as pens and paper.
- A list of animal characters and their traits.

Activity

1. Introduce the activity to the class, emphasizing the use of animal characters to represent people and their behaviors.
2. Provide the students with a list of animal characters and their traits to

help them create their fable.

3. Have the students create a personal fable based on a personal experience or story,.

4. Once the fables are complete, have the students share them with the class,.

5. Encourage the students to compare and contrast their fables, focusing on similarities and differences between the different animal characters and their behaviours.

6. Have the students discuss the morals of their fables and the importance of storytelling in conveying messages and lessons.

Extension

- Ask the students to create illustrations or animations to accompany their fables.
- Have the students present their fables as a play or puppet show,.

Alternatives

- You could ask the students to create a group fable, emphasizing collaboration and teamwork in storytelling.
- You could ask the students to analyze and compare different fables, focusing on the use of animal characters and their representation of people and their behaviors.

29

Picture Storytelling

Preparation

- Find an appropriate picture book story, or print out a similar story.

Materials

- Picture book.

Activity

1. Introduce the picture book and ask the students to make predictions about the story.
2. Begin reading the story aloud, using the target language frequently.
3. After a few pages, stop and ask the students to predict what will happen next.
4. Continue reading the story, pausing regularly to ask questions and encourage discussion.
5. When you finish the story, ask the students to retell it in their own words, using as much of the target language as possible.
6. Have the students work in pairs or small groups to create their own

stories using the pictures from the book.

Extension

- Have the students write their own ending to the story.
- Ask the students to create a storyboard for a new story using the same characters.

Alternatives

- Instead of using a picture book, you provide the students with pictures and ask them to create their own stories.
- You could ask the students to create a story based on a single picture.

30

Proverb Stories

Preparation

- Introduce the concept of proverbs and their use of concise and memorable sayings to convey a message or lesson.
- Provide examples of proverbs and their meanings to the class.
- Ask the students to choose a proverb they like and think about how they can create a story around it.
- Provide the students with a list of storytelling techniques, such as plot development, character development, and imagery.

Materials

- Writing materials, such as pens and paper.
- A list of proverbs and their meanings.
- A list of storytelling techniques.

Activity

1. Provide the students with a list of proverbs and their meanings to help them choose a proverb they like.
2. Have the students create a story around their chosen proverb,.
3. Once the stories are complete, have the students share them with the class,.
4. Encourage the students to compare and contrast their stories, focusing on the use of the chosen proverb and the storytelling techniques used.
5. Have the students discuss the message or lesson conveyed in their stories and the importance of proverbs in storytelling.

Extension

- Ask the students to create illustrations or animations to accompany their stories,.
- Have the students present their stories as a play or puppet show,.

Alternatives

- You could ask the students to create a group story, emphasizing collaboration and teamwork in storytelling.
- You could ask the students to analyze and compare different proverbs.

31

Scavenger Hunt

Preparation

1. Prepare a list of clues related to the story, emphasizing the target language.

Materials

- Paper, pencils, and any props or objects related to the story.

Activity

1. Divide the class into small groups and explain that they will go on a scavenger hunt related to the story.
2. Provide each group with a list of clues related to the story, emphasizing the use of the target language in their responses.
3. Allow the groups to search for the objects or props related to the story, using the clues provided.
4. Let each group present their findings to the class, emphasizing the use of the target language in their descriptions.

Extension

- Ask the students to write a new scene to the story and create a scavenger hunt related to the new scene, emphasizing the target language in the clues.
- Have the students work in pairs or small groups to retell the story in their own words, using as much of the target language as possible.

Alternatives

- Instead of using props or objects related to the story, you could provide the students with pictures or images, asking them to search for clues related to the story in the pictures.
- You could ask the students to create their own clues for a scavenger hunt related to the story.

32

Shadow Play

Preparation

1. Prepare materials for making shadow puppets such as black paper, scissors, and sticks.

Materials

- Black paper, scissors, sticks, a large white sheet, a strong light source, and any other materials students may want to use to create their shadow puppets.

Activity

1. Explain to the students that they will create a shadow play related to the story, emphasizing the target language.
2. Provide the students with materials for making shadow puppets, and ask them to plan and create their shadow puppets based on the characters in the story, emphasizing the use of the target language in their planning and descriptions.
3. Allow the students to work on their shadow puppets, providing support

and guidance as needed, and emphasizing the use of the target language in their discussions and explanations.

4. Set up a large white sheet and a strong light source, and have the students perform their shadow play behind the sheet, emphasizing the use of the target language in their storytelling.

Extension

- Ask the students to write a new scene to the story and create a new set of shadow puppets related to the scene, emphasizing the target language.
- Have the students work in pairs or small groups to retell the story in their own words, using as much of the target language as possible.

Alternatives

- Instead of creating a shadow play, you could ask the students to create a stop-motion animation related to the story.
- You could ask the students to create their own shadow plays or stop-motion animations related to the story or a new scene.

33

Serial Storytelling

Preparation

1. Choose a story suitable for serialization, ensuring that it has a straight-forward plot and is appropriate for the level and interests of the students.
2. Divide the story into several parts, ensuring each part suits a single class session.

Materials

- Copies of the story for each student.

Activity

1. Begin by introducing the story to the class.
2. Read the first part of the story to the class.
3. Have the students discuss the story so far, focusing on the plot, characters, and language use.
4. Divide the class into small groups, and assign each group a different aspect of the story to focus on, such as the characters, setting, or language use.

5. Have each group present their findings to the class.
6. Once each group has presented, continue reading the next part of the story.
7. Repeat the process for each subsequent part of the story, focusing on different aspects of the story.
8. Once the story is complete, have the class discuss what they liked and what could be improved about the story.

Extension

- Ask the students to write their own continuation or alternate ending to the story.
- Have the students create illustrations or animations to accompany their retelling of the story.

Alternatives

- You could ask the students to act out different parts of the story.
- You could ask the students to compare and contrast different aspects of the story.

34

Song Activity

Preparation

1. Find a song related to the story.

Materials

- Musical instruments or a recorded version of the song.

Activity

1. Explain to the students that they will create a song related to the story, emphasizing the target language.
2. Provide the students with musical instruments or a recorded version of the song.
3. Encourage the students to brainstorm lyrics related to the story, emphasizing the use of the target language in their lyrics.
4. Allow the students to work together to create their song, emphasizing the use of the target language in their lyrics and performance.
5. Let each group present their song to the class, emphasizing the use of the target language in their performance.

Extension

- Ask the students to create a music video related to the story and their song, emphasizing the use of the target language in their lyrics and video.
- Have the students work in pairs or small groups to retell the story in their own words, using as much of the target language as possible.

Alternatives

- Instead of creating a new song, you could provide the students with a well-known song and ask them to write new lyrics related to the story.
- You could provide the students with different musical styles and ask them to create songs related to the story in those different styles.

35

Story Circle

Preparation

1. Prepare a story that is appropriate for your students' level and interests.
2. Identify the target language you want to focus on in the story.

Materials

- None required.

Activity

1. Have the students sit in a circle.
2. Begin telling the story, using the target language frequently.
3. After a few sentences or a paragraph, stop and choose a student to continue the story.
4. Continue around the circle, with each student adding to the story in turn.
5. Encourage the students to listen carefully.

Extensions

- Ask the students to write their own ending to the story.
- Have the students work in pairs or small groups to retell the story in their own words, using as much of the target language as possible.

Alternatives

- Instead of having the students tell a story together, you could tell the story and ask the students to listen for specific information or language structures.
- You could provide the students with pictures and ask them to create a story using the target language.

<h1 style="text-align:center">36</h1>

Story Cube

Preparation

1. Create a cube with pictures or phrases related to the story, emphasizing the target language.

Materials

- A cube with pictures or phrases related to the story, paper, pencils.

Activity

1. Explain to the students that they will use a cube to create a story related to the story, emphasizing the target language.
2. Provide the students with a cube with pictures or phrases related to the story.
3. Encourage the students to roll the cube and use the picture or phrase they land on to create a new part of the story.
4. Allow the students to take turns rolling the cube and adding to the story, emphasizing the use of the target language in their responses.
5. Let the students share their stories with the class, emphasizing the use

of the target language in their descriptions and storytelling.

Extension

- Ask the students to write a new scene to the story and create a new cube with pictures or phrases related to the new scene, emphasizing the target language.
- Have the students work in pairs or small groups to retell the story in their own words, using as much of the target language as possible.

Alternatives

- Instead of creating a cube, you could give the students a deck of cards or another randomization tool with pictures or phrases related to the story.
- You could ask the students to create their own cubes or randomization tools related to the story or a new scene.

37

Story Debate

Preparation

1. Prepare a list of debate topics related to the story, or character cards if choosing to assign characters.

Materials

- List of debate topics, character cards

Activity

1. Divide the class into two teams, one in favour of the story and the other against it. If you wish, you could assign characters from the story to students in each group.
2. Explain to the students that they will debate the story's merits, focusing on the target language.
3. Provide each team with a list of debate topics related to the story, emphasizing the use of the target language in their arguments.
4. Allow each team time to prepare their arguments and rebuttals, emphasizing the use of the target language.

5. Let each team present their arguments, with the other team providing rebuttals and counterarguments.
6. Encourage the students to use the target language as much as possible to help them develop their language skills.

Extension

- Ask the students to write a new scene to the story and debate its merits, using the target language to support their arguments.
- Have the students work in pairs or small groups to retell the story in their own words, using as much of the target language as possible.

Alternatives

- Instead of dividing the class into two teams, you could assign different debate roles to each student, such as moderator, debater, or timekeeper.

38

Story Dominoes

Preparation

1. Choose a series of picture cards or images that represent different elements of a story, such as characters, settings, and objects.
2. Introduce the concept of storytelling and its importance in language learning.
3. Provide examples of storytelling techniques, such as character development, plot development, and imagery.

Materials

- A set of picture cards or images.
- Writing materials, such as pens and paper.
- A list of storytelling techniques.

Activity

1. Explain the rules of the activity: each student will take turns putting down a picture card and using it to create the next part of the story.
2. Start the story with a simple sentence or a character description, depend-

ing on the picture card chosen.

3. Have the students take turns putting down a picture card and use it to create the next part of the story.

4. Encourage the students to use the list of storytelling techniques to create a well-developed story.

5. Once the story is complete, have the students read it aloud.

6. Encourage the students to compare and contrast the different picture cards and their impact on the story.

Extension

- Ask the students to create illustrations or animations to accompany their story.
- Have the students present their story as a play or puppet show.

Alternatives

- You could ask the students to create a group story.

<h1 style="text-align:center">39</h1>

<h1 style="text-align:center">Story Quiz</h1>

Preparation

1. Prepare a list of sample quiz questions related to the story, emphasizing the target language.

Materials

- Paper, pencils, and any props or objects related to the story.

Activity

1. Divide the class into pairs and explain that they will create a quiz related to the story for their partner to answer.
2. Provide each pair with paper and pencils and encourage them to create their own quiz questions, using the sample questions provided as a guide.
3. Allow the pairs time to create their quiz questions, emphasizing the use of the target language in their questions and responses.
4. Let each pair exchange their quizzes with their partner and answer the questions, emphasizing the use of the target language in their responses.

Extension

- Ask the students to write a new scene to the story and create a quiz related to the new scene, emphasizing the target language in their questions and responses.
- Have the students work in pairs or small groups to retell the story in their own words, using as much of the target language as possible.

Alternatives

- Instead of a pre-written story, you could ask the students to create their own story and quiz questions, emphasizing their creativity and language skills.
- You could provide the students with different quiz formats, such as multiple-choice or fill-in-the-blank.

40

Story Roleplay

Preparation

1. Prepare role cards or prompts for each student with a character description, including their background, personality, and motivations.

Materials

- Role cards or prompts.

Activity

1. Divide the class into small groups, with each student assigned a role.
2. Explain to the students that they will act out the story from the perspective of their assigned character.
3. Give students time to prepare their roles, focusing on developing their language use and vocabulary.
4. Let each group perform their roleplay for the class, using props or costumes to help bring the story to life.
5. Encourage students to use the target language as much as possible, to help them develop their language skills.

Extensions

- Ask the students to rewrite the story from a different character's perspective, using the target language to describe their thoughts, feelings, and motivations.
- Have the students work in pairs or small groups to retell the story in their own words, using as much of the target language as possible.

Alternatives

- Instead of assigning specific roles, you could ask the students to improvise their own roles based on the story.
- You could provide the students with prompts or sentence starters.

41

Stories from Students

Preparation

1. Think of several topics or themes that students would be interested in, that could naturally incorporate the target language.

Materials

- Whiteboard, markers, any props or visuals prepared by you or the students.

Activity

1. Ask each student to share their story with the class.
2. After each story, have the class discuss what they liked and what could be improved.
3. Encourage the students to ask questions and provide feedback to each other.
4. As the stories progress, have the students illustrate the stories on the whiteboard or with props and visuals.
5. Let the students vote on their favorite story.
6. Provide feedback to each student on their storytelling skills and language

use.

Extension

- Have the students work in pairs or small groups to develop a longer story, using as much of the target language as possible.
- Ask the students to write their stories and publish them in a class book or on a class website.

Alternatives

- You could provide a prompt for each student to base their story on.
- You could ask the students to work in pairs or small groups to develop a story based on a picture or a series of pictures.

42

Storytelling Boxes

Preparation

1. Choose a box and select several objects to place inside.
2. Prepare a list of storytelling techniques, such as character development, plot development, and imagery.
3. Introduce the concept of storytelling and its importance in language learning.

Materials

- A box filled with objects.
- Writing materials, such as pens and paper.
- A list of storytelling techniques.

Activity

1. Show the box to the students and ask them to guess what might be inside.
2. Have the students take turns choosing an object from the box.
3. Ask the students to create a story based on the object they have chosen, emphasizing the use of the target language in their storytelling and

descriptions.

4. Encourage the students to use the list of storytelling techniques to create a well-developed story.
5. Once the stories are complete, have the students share them with the class.
6. Encourage the students to compare and contrast their stories.
7. Have the students discuss the importance of objects in storytelling and the role of imagination in creating a story.

Extension

- Ask the students to create illustrations or animations to accompany their stories, emphasizing the use of the target language in their descriptions and explanations.
- Have the students present their stories as a play or puppet show,.

Alternatives

- You could ask the students to create a group story, emphasizing collaboration and teamwork in storytelling.
- You could ask the students to analyze and compare different objects.

43

Storytelling with Video

Preparation

1. Prepare a script or storyboard for the video, highlighting the target language.

Materials

- Video camera or smartphone, computer, and video editing software.

Activity

1. Divide the class into small groups, each assigned a different part of the story.
2. Explain to the students that they will create a video to retell their part of the story, using as much of the target language as possible.
3. Give each group a video camera or smartphone and allow them to plan and film their part of the story, emphasizing the use of the target language in their dialogue and narration.
4. Let the groups edit their video using video editing software, adding titles, captions, and sound effects.

5. Let each group share their video with the class, retelling their part of the story using the target language.

6. Encourage the students to provide feedback on each other's work, focusing on language use, creativity, and technical aspects of the video production.

Extension

- Ask the students to write a new scene to the story and film it in a new video.
- Have the students work in pairs or small groups to retell the entire story in video format, using as much of the target language as possible.

Alternatives

- Instead of assigning different parts of the story to each group, you could provide the students with a script or storyboard and ask them to create their own version of the story in video format, using the target language.
- You could ask the students to create a silent video.

44

Student Podcast

Preparation

1. Prepare materials for making an audio drama or podcast, such as a recording device, editing software, and background music.

Materials

- A recording device, editing software, background music, and any other materials students may want to use to create their audio drama or podcast.

Activity

1. Explain to the students that they will create an audio drama or podcast related to the story, emphasizing the target language.
2. Divide the students into groups, and assign roles such as actors, writers, and sound engineers.
3. Provide the students with time to plan and write their script, emphasizing the use of the target language in their writing and dialogue.
4. Allow the students to record their audio drama or podcast, providing support and guidance as needed.

5. Let the students listen to each other's audio dramas or podcasts and provide feedback on each other's work.

Alternatives

- Instead of creating an audio drama or podcast, you could ask the students to create a radio news show related to the story.
- You could ask the students to create their own audio dramas or podcasts related to the story or a new scene.

Extension

- Ask the students to write a new scene to the story and create a new audio drama or podcast related to the scene.
- Have the students work in pairs or small groups to retell the story in their own words, using as much of the target language as possible.

45

Treasure Hunt

Preparation

1. Choose a story that is suitable for the activity.
2. Create clues that will lead the students to different locations or objects related to the story.

Materials

- Copies of the story for each student.
- Writing materials, such as pens and paper.
- Clues or scavenger hunt items related to the story.

Activity

1. Divide the class into small groups and give each group a clue related to the story.
2. Have the students work together to decipher the clue and find the location or object related to the story.
3. Once the group has found the location or object, have them retell the part of the story related to the clue.

4. Repeat the process for each subsequent clue.

Extension

- Ask the students to write their own continuation or alternate ending to the story.
- Have the students create illustrations or animations to accompany their retelling of the story.

Alternatives

- You could ask the students to create their own clues related to the story.
- You could ask the students to act out different parts of the story related to each clue.

46

Treasure Map

Preparation

1. Create a map of the story with key locations, emphasizing the target language.

Materials

- Paper and pencils, a large blank map or a digital map-making tool.

Activity

1. Explain to the students that they will create a map of the story, emphasizing the target language.
2. Provide the students with a blank map or a digital map-making tool and ask them to label the key locations in the story, using the target language in their labels.
3. Allow the students to add details to the map as they read or hear more of the story, emphasizing the use of the target language in their descriptions and explanations.
4. Let the students share their maps with the class and discuss how the

locations relate to the story, emphasizing the use of the target language in their descriptions and storytelling.

Extension:

- Ask the students to write a new scene to the story and add related locations to the map, emphasizing the target language.
- Have the students work in pairs or small groups to retell the story in their own words, using as much of the target language as possible.

Alternatives

- Instead of creating a map, you could ask the students to create a 3D model of a key location in the story.
- You could ask the students to create their own maps or 3D models related to the story or a new scene, encouraging them to develop their creativity and language skills in different ways.

47

Turn-Taking Story

Preparation

1. None needed.

Materials

- None needed.

Activity

1. Begin telling the story to the class, but stop before the end of a key event or plot point.
2. Ask the students what they think should happen next, emphasizing the use of the target language in their responses.
3. Use the students' suggestions to continue the story, but stop again before another key event or plot point ends.
4. Ask the students what they think should happen next.
5. Continue telling the story this way, taking turns with the students to develop the plot.
6. Once the story is complete, have the class discuss what they liked and

what could be improved about the story.

Extension

- Have the students work in pairs or small groups to create their own turn-taking stories.
- Ask the students to write an alternative ending or a sequel to the story.

Alternatives

- You could ask the students to work in pairs or small groups to create a story, but each student can only add one sentence at a time.
- You could ask the students to create a visual representation of the story.
- This activity could be a dictation activity to practice writing – so the students write all of the story as you read it, then add their own part.

48

Two Truths and a Lie

Preparation

- None needed.

Materials

- None needed.

Activity

1. Explain to the class the game's rules, "Two Truths and a Lie," where each person tells three statements about themselves, two of which are true and one of which is a lie.
2. Have each student come up with two true statements and one false statement about a specific topic, such as a favourite hobby or a memorable vacation.
3. Encourage the students to use descriptive and vivid language in their statements to make them more engaging and entertaining.
4. Have each student take turns sharing their statements with the class.
5. After each student has shared their statements, have the class try to guess

which statement was false.

6. Continue playing until each student has had a turn.
7. Have the class discuss what they liked and what could be improved about the stories

Extension

- Ask the students to work in pairs or small groups to create a story using the true statements they shared in the game.
- Have the students create illustrations or animations to accompany their story.

Alternatives

- You could ask the students to create a character or a scene based on their true statements.
- You could ask the students to play the game using a specific set of vocabulary or grammar structures.

49

Word Ladder

Preparation

1. Create a list of related vocabulary words or phrases to the story, emphasizing the target language.

Materials

- Paper and pencils.

Activity

1. Explain to the students that they will play a word ladder game related to the story, emphasizing the target language.
2. Provide the students with a list of related vocabulary words or phrases to the story, emphasizing the use of the target language in their responses.
3. Choose a starting word related to the story and ask the students to write down a new word related to the story that starts with the last letter of the previous word.
4. Allow the students to take turns writing down a new word related to the story and the previous word, emphasizing the use of the target language

in their responses.

5. Let the students continue the word ladder game until they can no longer think of new words or phrases related to the story.

Extension

- Ask the students to write a new scene to the story and create a new list of related vocabulary words or phrases to the new scene, emphasizing the target language.
- Have the students work in pairs or small groups to retell the story in their own words, using as much of the target language as possible.

Alternatives

- Instead of providing a list of related vocabulary words or phrases, you could provide the students with pictures or images related to the story and ask them to come up with a new word or phrase related to the story and the previous word
- You could ask the students to create their own word ladder games related to the story or a new scene.

V

Final Thoughts

50

Storytelling Challenges

A word of warning - there's no perfect way to teach a language, and using stories is no exception.

Incorporating storytelling into language teaching can be a highly effective and engaging approach. However, it is not without its challenges. Let's look at common challenges you might face when using stories in your lessons and how to overcome them.

Preserve the magic of stories

If stories are used solely as a tool to practice vocabulary or grammar, their magic and appeal may be lost. To prevent this, ensure that activities related to the story remain fun and engaging, and allow students to immerse themselves in the storytelling process without excessive interruptions. Striking the right balance between storytelling and learning is essential.

Select stories with appropriate language level

Choosing stories that match the language proficiency of your students is crucial. Opt for stories that are suitable for their level, and simplify the language if necessary. This ensures that students can understand the story and effectively retain the language they are learning.

Balancing storytelling with teaching

To provide a well-rounded language education, it is important to balance storytelling with other traditional language instruction methods, such as grammar and vocabulary lessons. This equips students with the necessary skills to understand and use the language in real-life situations.

Encouraging student participation

Active student participation is key to a successful storytelling experience. Prompt students to ask questions, engage in role-playing activities, and apply the language they have learned to comprehend the story. This fosters engagement and boosts their confidence in using the language.

Avoiding over-reliance on a single storytelling technique

Using the same setup or technique repeatedly may cause students to lose interest. To maintain engagement, vary the storytelling techniques and activities employed in the classroom. Experiment with different approaches, such as visual aids, props, or interactive activities to keep the learning experience fresh and exciting.

Ensuring authenticity in storytelling

Stories that lack a clear direction or feel artificial can diminish the storytelling experience. To avoid this, carefully select stories with meaningful content and deliver them with genuine emotion and enthusiasm. Remember, authenticity is key, as students can easily detect insincerity in storytelling.

Overcoming these storytelling challenges is crucial for you when aiming to create an effective and engaging learning environment. By being mindful of these potential obstacles and actively working to address them, you can maximize the benefits of storytelling in your language lessons and provide a rich and immersive learning experience for your students.

51

Become a Master Storyteller

Mastering the art of storytelling is an essential skill for language teachers.

By engaging your students with captivating stories, you can create an interactive and enjoyable learning environment that fosters language acquisition and retention. Let's look at the various techniques to enhance your storytelling abilities and help you become a master storyteller in the classroom.

Use visual aids

Incorporating visual aids such as images, illustrations, and videos can help bring the story to life and make it more memorable for students. These visual elements can also support comprehension by providing context and reinforcing key vocabulary and concepts.

Embrace the 'campfire style'

Creating an intimate and cozy atmosphere by sitting around in a circle can make storytelling sessions more engaging and enjoyable for students. This informal setting can encourage open discussion and help students feel more connected to the story and each other.

Foster excitement and anticipation

Maintain a sense of wonder and enthusiasm when sharing stories with your students. Build anticipation by giving them a taste of what's to come or by introducing a storytelling tradition, such as a special phrase or gesture to signal the beginning of a story.

Separate storytelling and analysis

Be upfront with your students about the distinction between enjoying the story and analyzing it. Encourage them to relax, listen, and enjoy the story first, then discuss or work on related activities afterwards.

Provide student support and differentiation

Tailor your storytelling sessions to suit the needs and abilities of your students. This may involve using different materials, visual aids, or boardwork during the storytelling process to accommodate various learning styles and preferences.

Encourage creativity and warm-up activities

It can be challenging for students to generate stories on the spot. To help them become more comfortable with storytelling, introduce fun and engaging warm-up activities that promote creativity, such as brainstorming sessions, role-playing games, or collaborative story-building exercises.

Vary the pace

Adjusting the pace of your storytelling, from slow and deliberate to fast-paced and energetic, can help maintain student interest and engagement. Experiment with different storytelling rhythms, tones, and styles to find what works best for you and your students.

Utilize storytelling props

Props such as puppets, masks, and toy figures can add an extra dimension to your storytelling sessions, making them more dynamic and memorable. These tangible items can also help students visualize the story's characters and settings more vividly.

Encourage student-generated stories

Prompt students to create their own stories based on the themes or characters in the story you've shared. This can help them internalize the language, feel more invested in the learning process, and develop their own storytelling skills.

Make connections to real life

Linking the story to real-life situations can help students better understand the narrative and feel more motivated to learn. Draw parallels between the story's themes or lessons and the students' experiences, encouraging them to reflect on how these connections relate to their lives.

When you incorporate these strategies, you can elevate your storytelling skills and create a rich and engaging language-learning experience for your students. Remember, the key to becoming a master storyteller is to continuously experiment, adapt, and grow as both a teacher and a storyteller.

Notes

WHY STORIES?

1   Haidt, J. (ed.) (2013) *The righteous mind: why good people are divided by politics and religion*. 1. Vintage books ed. New York: Vintage Books.

THE SCIENCE OF STORYTELLING

2   Schank, R.C. and Abelson, R.P. (1995), "Knowledge and memory: the real story", in Wyer Jr., R.S. (ed.), Advances in social cognition. Volume VIII, Hillsdale, Lawrence Erlbaum Associates, 1(85).

3   Lugossy, R. (2006), "Shaping teachers' beliefs through narratives", in Nikolov, M. and Horvath, J. (eds.), UPRT 2006: empirical studies in English applied linguistics, Pécs, Lingua Franca Csoport, 329(352).

4   Brewster, J., Ellis, G., and Girard, D. (2002). The Primary English Teacher's Guide. England: Penguin.

5   Brewster, J., Ellis, G. and Girard, D. (2002), The primary English teacher's guide, England, Penguin.

6   Elley, W.B. (1989) 'Vocabulary Acquisition from Listening to Stories', *Reading Research Quarterly*, 24(2), pp. 174–187. Available at: https://doi.org/10.2307/747863.

7   Sentürk, S. and Kahraman, A. (2020) 'The Use of Short Stories in English Language Teaching and Its Benefits on Grammar Learning', *International Journal of Curriculum and Instruction*, 12(2), pp. 533–559.

8   Abdolmanafi-Rokni, S.J. (2013) 'The Effect of Listening to Audio Stories on Pronunciation of EFL Learners'.

9   Vivas, E. (1996) 'Effects of Story Reading on Language', *Language Learning*, 46(2), pp. 189–216. Available at: https://doi.org/10.1111/j.1467-1770.1996.tb01234.x.

10 Elley, W.B. and Mangubhai, F. (1983) 'The Impact of Reading on Second Language Learning', *Reading Research Quarterly*, 19(1), p. 53. Available at: https://doi.org/10.2307/747337.

11 Bartan, Ö.Ş., 2017. The effects of reading short stories in improving foreign language writing skills. *The Reading Matrix: An International Online Journal*, 17(1), pp.59-74.

12 Duff, A. and Maley, A. (2007). Literature. (Second edition). Oxford: Oxford University Press.

13 Nikolov, M. and Languages, E.C. for M. (2007) *Teaching Modern Languages to Young Learners: Teachers, Curricula and Materials*. Council of Europe.

14 Phillips, L. (2000) 'Storytelling: The Seeds of Children's Creativity', *Australasian Journal of Early Childhood*, 25(3), pp. 1–5. Available at: https://doi.org/10.1177/183693910002500302.

15 Nation, P. (2000) 'Learning Vocabulary in Lexical Sets: Dangers and Guidelines', *TESOL Journal*, 9. Available at: https://doi.org/10.1002/j.1949-3533.2000.tb00239.x.

STORY FRAMEWORKS

16 Joseph Campbell, *The Hero with a Thousand Faces*. Princeton: Princeton University Press, 1949

A STORY-PLANNING METHOD

17 Weller, D. (2019) *Lesson Planning for Language Teachers: Evidence-Based Techniques for Busy Teachers*. Independently published.

About the Author

I'm David Weller - a TEFL teacher, trainer, manager and insatiable coffee drinker.

I started teaching in 2003, and since then, I've been a teacher, trainer, manager, regional manager, examiner, moderator and just about everything else. Along the way, I've also completed the Trinity DipTESOL and a Master's in TESOL. I think it's fair to say that I will be working in education for life.

If you'd like to keep in touch, sign up for my free, twice-monthly newsletter at barefootTEFLteacher.com - you can read the old newsletters there, too.

Thanks for reading, and the best of luck with your teaching journey.

Subscribe to my newsletter:

✉ https://www.barefootteflteacher.com

Also by David Weller

Lesson Planning for Language Teachers

Do you want to plan better, faster and worry-free?

Most of the time, planning sucks. It takes ages, and your next lesson is in thirty minutes.

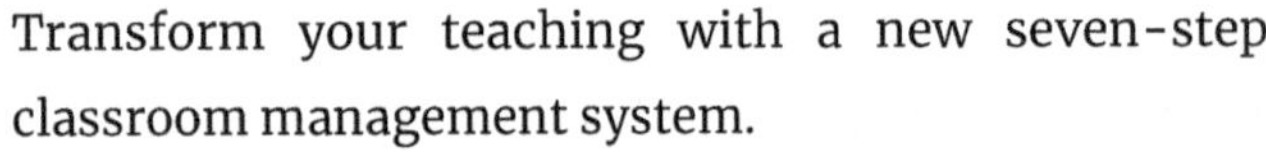

You CAN finish your planning faster, with awesome activities, and still have time to chat in the staffroom. Read this to find out how.

Essential Classroom Management

Transform your teaching with a new seven-step classroom management system.

It's the key to a calm class, a relaxed mind, and a classroom full of learning.

Reflective Teaching Journal

Do you want to be an amazing teacher AND have a work-life balance?

Follow this guided reflective journal for just five minutes a day to get more control, confidence and clarity in your teaching.